Succeed on the Standardized Test

This Book Includes:

- 2 Performance Based Assessments (PBA)
- 2 End-Of-Year (EOY) Assessments
- Detailed Answer explanations for every question
- Type I questions - Concepts, Skills and Procedures
  Type II questions - Expressing Mathematical Reasoning
  Type III questions - Modeling and/or Applications
- Strategies for building speed and accuracy
- Content aligned with the new Common Core State Standards

Plus access to Online Workbooks which include:

- Hundreds of practice questions
- Self-paced learning and personalized score reports
- Instant feedback after completion of the workbook

Complement Classroom Learning All Year

Using the Lumos Study Program, parents and teachers can reinforce the classroom learning experience for children. It creates a collaborative learning platform for students, teachers and parents.

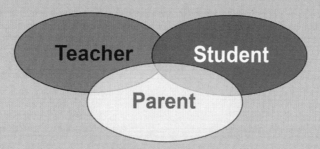

Used in Schools and Public Libraries
To Improve Student Achievement

Lumos Learning

Common Core Assessments and Online Workbooks: Grade 4 Mathematics, PARCC Edition

Contributing Editor	-	**Krista Clowers**
Contributing Editor	-	**George Smith**
Contributing Editor	-	**Gregory Applegate**
Curriculum Director	-	**Marisa Adams**
Executive Producer	-	**Mukunda Krishnaswamy**
Illustrator		- **Mirona Jova**
Designer		- **Raghavendra Rao R.**

ISBN-10: 1940484197

ISBN-13: 978-1-940484-19-8

Printed in the United States of America

For permissions and additional information contact us

Lumos Information Services, LLC
PO Box 1575, Piscataway, NJ 08855-1575
http://www.LumosLearning.com

Email: support@lumoslearning.com
Tel: (732) 384-0146
Fax: (866) 283-6471

Lumos Learning

Table of Contents

Introduction

The Common Core State Standards Initiative (CCSS) was created from the need to have more robust and rigorous guidelines, which could be standardized from state to state. These guidelines create a learning environment where students will be able to graduate high school with all skills necessary to be active and successful members of society, whether they take a role in the workforce or in some sort of post-secondary education.

Once the CCSS were fully developed and implemented, it became necessary to devise a way to ensure they were assessed appropriately. To this end, states adopting the CCSS have joined one of two consortia, either PARCC or Smarter Balanced.

What is PARCC?

The Partnership for Assessment of Readiness for College and Careers (PARCC) is one of the two state consortiums responsible for developing assessments aligned to the new, more rigorous Common Core State Standards. A combination of educational leaders from PARCC Governing and Participating states, along with test developers, have worked together to create the new computer based English Language Arts and Math Assessments.

PARCC has spent the better part of two years developing their new assessments, and in many ways, they will be unlike anything many students have ever seen. The tests will be conducted online, requiring students to complete tasks to assess a deeper understanding of the CCSS. Additionally, instead of one final test at the end of the year, PARCC understands that the best way to measure student success is to assess them multiple times a year. So, students in PARCC states will take a mid-year assessment called a Performance Based Assessment (PBA) and an End-of-Year Assessment (EOY).

How Can the Lumos Study Program Prepare Students for PARCC Tests?

Beginning in the fall of 2014, student mastery of Common Core State Standards will be assessed using standardized testing methods. At Lumos Learning, we believe that year-long learning and adequate practice before the actual test are the keys to success on these standardized tests. We have designed the Lumos study program to help students get plenty of realistic practice before the test and to promote year long collaborative learning.

This is a Lumos **tedBook**™. It connects you to Online Workbooks and additional resources using a number of devices including Android phones, iPhones, tablets and personal computers. The Lumos StepUp Online Workbooks are designed to promote year-long learning. It is a simple program students can securely access using a computer or device with internet access. It consists of hundreds of grade appropriate questions, aligned to the new Common Core State Standards. Students will get instant feedback and can review their answers anytime. Each student's answers and progress can be reviewed by parents and educators to reinforce the learning experience.

LumosLearning.com

How to use this book effectively

The Lumos Program is a flexible learning tool. It can be adapted to suit a student's skill level and the time available to practice before standardized tests. Here are some tips to help you use this book and the online workbooks effectively:

Students
- Take one Performance Based Assessment (PBA).
- Use the "Related Lumos StepUp™ Online Workbook" in the Answer Key section to identify the topic that is related to each question.
- Use the Online workbooks to practice your areas of difficulty and complement classroom learning.
- Download the Lumos StepUp™ app using the instructions provided in Lumos StepUp™ Mobile App FAQ to have anywhere access to online resources.
- Have open-ended questions evaluated by a teacher or parent, keeping in mind the scoring rubrics.
- Take the second PBA as you get close to the test date.
- Complete the test in a quiet place, following the test guidelines. Practice tests provide you an opportunity to improve your test-taking skills and to review topics included in the PARCC test.
- As the end of the year becomes closer, take one EOY and follow the above guidelines before taking the second.

Parents
- Familiarize yourself with the PARCC test format and expectations.
- Help your child use Lumos StepUp™ Online Workbooks by following the instructions in "How to access the Lumos Online Workbooks" section of this chapter.
- Download the Lumos SchoolUp™ app using the instructions provided in the Lumos SchoolUp™ Mobile App FAQ section of this chapter to get useful school information.
- Review your child's performance in the "Lumos Online Workbooks" periodically. You can do this by simply asking your child to log into the system online and select the subject area you wish to review.
- Review your child's work in the practice PBA's and EOY's.

Teachers
- Please contact **support@lumoslearning.com** to request a **teacher account.** A teacher account will help you create custom assessments and lessons as well as review the online work of your students. Visit **http://www.lumoslearning.com/math-quill** to learn more.
- Download the Lumos SchoolUp™ app using the instructions provided in Lumos SchoolUp™ Mobile App FAQ to get convenient access to Common Core State Standards and additional school related resources.
- If your school has purchased the school edition of this book, please use this book as the Teacher Guide.
- You can use the Lumos online programs along with this book to complement and extend your classroom instruction.

PARCC Frequently Asked Questions

What Will PARCC Math Assessment Look Like?

For Math, PARCC differentiates three different types of questions:

Type I – Tasks assessing concepts, skills, procedures (Machine scorable only)
- Balance of conceptual understanding, fluency, and application
- Can involve any or all mathematical practice standards
- Machine scorable including innovative, computer-based formats
- Will appear on the End of Year and Performance Based Assessment components

Type II - Tasks assessing expressing mathematical reasoning
- Each task calls for written arguments/justifications, critique of reasoning or precision in mathematical statements (MP.3, 6).
- Can involve other mathematical practice standards
- May include a mix of machine-scored and hand-scored responses
- Included on the Performance Based Assessment component

Type III - Tasks assessing modeling/applications
- Each task calls for modeling/application in a real-world context or scenario (MP.4)
- Can involve other mathematical practice standards
- May include a mix of machine-scored and hand-scored responses
- Included on the Performance Based Assessment component

The PBA will be administered once 75% of the school year is complete. It will consist of Type I, Type II, and Type III questions. In the PBA, students will be given a set amount of time to complete their tasks.

The time for each PBA is described below:

Estimated Time on Task in Minutes (PBA)		
Grade	Session One	Session Two
3	50	50
4	50	50
5	50	50
6	50	50
7	50	50
8	50	50

LumosLearning.com

The EOY will be administered once 90% of the school year is complete. It will consist of Type I questions only. In the EOY, students will also be given a set amount of time to complete their tasks.

The time for each EOY is described below:

Estimated Time on Task in Minutes (EOY)		
Grade	Session One	Session Two
3	55	55
4	55	55
5	55	55
6	55	55
7	55	55
8	55	55

What is a PARCC Aligned Test Practice Book?

Inside this book, you will find four full-length practice tests that are similar to the standardized tests students will take to assess their mastery of CCSS-aligned curriculum. Completing these tests will help students master the different areas that are included in newly aligned standardized tests and practice test taking skills. The results will help the students and educators get insights into students' strengths and weaknesses in specific content areas. These insights could be used to help students strengthen their skills in difficult topics and to improve speed and accuracy while taking the test.

How is this Lumos tedBook aligned to PARCC Guidelines?

Although the PARCC assessments will be conducted online, the practice tests here have been created to accurately reflect the depth and rigor of PARCC tasks in a pencil and paper format. Students will still be exposed to the Technology Enhanced Constructed-Response (TECR) style questions so they become familiar with the wording and how to think through these types of tasks.

This edition of the practice test book was created in the Summer 2014 and aligned to the most current PARCC standards released to date. Some changes will occur as PARCC continues to release new information in the fall of 2014 and beyond.

Where can I get more information about PARCC?

You can obtain up-to-date information on PARCC, including sample assessment items, schedules, & the answers to frequently asked questions from the PARCC website at **http://www.parcconline.org**

Where can I get additional information about the Common Core State Standards (CCSS)?

Please visit **http://www.corestandards.org/Math**

How to access the Lumos Online Workbooks

First Time Access:

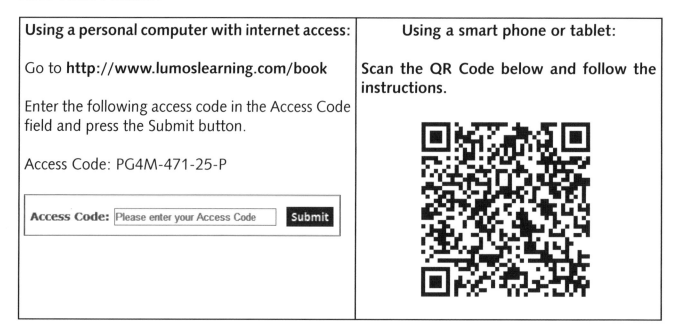

Using a personal computer with internet access:	Using a smart phone or tablet:
Go to **http://www.lumoslearning.com/book** Enter the following access code in the Access Code field and press the Submit button. Access Code: PG4M-471-25-P	Scan the QR Code below and follow the instructions.

In the next screen, click on the "New User" button to register your user name and password.

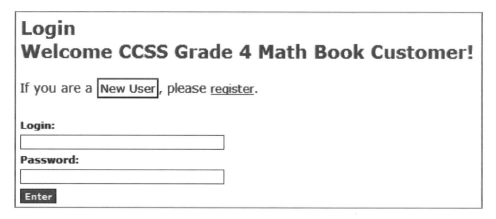

Subsequent Access:

After you establish your user id and password for subsequent access, simply login with your account information.

What if I buy more than one Lumos Study Program?
Please note that you can use all Online Workbooks with one User ID and Password. If you buy more than one book, you will access them with the same account.

Go back to the **http://www.lumoslearning.com/book** link and enter the access code provided in the second book. In the next screen simply login using your previously created account.

© Lumos Information Services 2014   LumosLearning.com

Lumos StepUp™ Mobile App FAQ For Students

What is the Lumos StepUp™ App?

It is a FREE application you can download onto your Android smart phones, tablets, iPhones, and iPads.

What are the Benefits of the StepUp™ App?

This mobile application gives convenient access to Common Core State Standards, Practice Tests, Online Workbooks, and learning resources through your smart phone and tablet computers.

Do I Need the StepUp™ App to Access Online Workbooks?

No, you can access Lumos StepUp™ Online Workbooks through a personal computer. The StepUp™ app simply enhances your learning experience and allows you to conveniently access StepUp™ Online Workbooks and additional resources through your smart phone or tablet.

How can I Download the App?

Visit **lumoslearning.com/a/stepup-app** using your smart phone or tablet and follow the instructions to download the app.

**QR Code
for Smart Phone
Or Tablet Users**

Lumos SchoolUp™ Mobile App FAQ For Parents

What is the Lumos SchoolUp™ App?

It is a FREE App that helps parents and teachers get a wide range of useful information about their school. It can be downloaded onto smartphones and tablets from popular App Stores.

What are the Benefits of the Lumos SchoolUp™ App?

It provides convenient access to

- School performance reports.
- School "Stickies". A Sticky could be information about an upcoming test, homework, extra curricular activities and other school events. Parents and educators can easily create their own sticky and share with the school community.
- Common Core State Standards.
- Sample questions.
- Educational blogs.
- StepUp™ student activity reports.

How can I Download the App?

Visit **lumoslearning.com/a/schoolup-app** using your smartphone or tablet and follow the instructions provided to download the App. Alternatively, scan the QR Code provided below using your smartphone or tablet computer.

**QR Code
for Smart Phone
Or Tablet Users**

Is SchoolUp™ available for Apple Devices?

SchoolUp™ would be available for Apple devices in the future. The initial release is supported on the Android platform. However, users with iPhones or iPads can use the web version of SchoolUp™ by logging on to **lumoslearning.com/a/schoolup**

     LumosLearning.com

Test Taking Tips

1) **The day before the test, make sure you get a good night's sleep.**

2) **On the day of the test, be sure to eat a good hearty breakfast! Also, be sure to arrive at school on time.**

3) **During the test:**

- **Read every question carefully.**

  - Do not spend too much time on any one question. Work steadily through all questions in the section.
  - Attempt all of the questions even if you are not sure of some answers.
  - If you run into a difficult question, eliminate as many choices as you can and then pick the best one from the remaining choices. Intelligent guessing will help you increase your score.
  - Also, mark the question so that if you have extra time, you can return to it after you reach the end of the section. Try to erase the marks after you complete the work.
  - Some questions may refer to a graph, chart, or other kind of picture. Carefully review the graphic before answering the question.
  - Be sure to include explanations for your written responses and show all work.

- **While Answering Multiple-Choice (EBSR) questions.**

  - Completely fill in the bubble corresponding to your answer choice.
  - Read all of the answer choices, even if think you have found the correct answer.

- **While Answering TECR questions.**

  - Read the directions of each question. Some might ask you to drag something, others to select, and still others to highlight. Follow all instructions of the question (or questions if it is in multiple parts)

Performance Based Assessment (PBA) - 1

Student Name:
Test Date:

Start Time:
End Time:

Here are some reminders for when you are taking the Grade 4 Mathematics Performance Based Assessment (PBA).

To answer the questions on the test, use the directions given in the question. If you do not know the answer to a question, skip it and go on to the next question. If time permits, you may return to questions in this session only. Do your best to answer every question.

---

1. Mrs. Brown's class has 4 pizzas that are all the exact same size and shape. If each pizza is cut into 8 equal slices and one slice is given to each student, how many slices of pizza will be left over after each of the 27 students gets a slice?

PART A

How many slices of pizza will be left over after each of the 27 students gets one slice?

	Slices

PART B

How do you know? Show or explain how you arrived at your answer.

© Lumos Information Services 2014   LumosLearning.com   ▲

2. **Enter your answer in the box.**

    Calculate the difference. 7,402 - 1,293 = [ ]

3. $\frac{9}{10}$ **is equivalent to what decimal?**

    Check the box above the decimal that is equivalent to $\frac{9}{10}$.

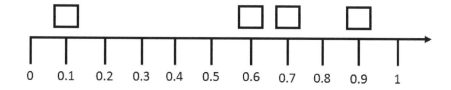

4. **Which figure models a line segment?**

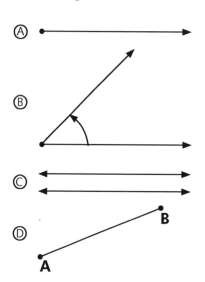

    Ⓐ
    Ⓑ
    Ⓒ
    Ⓓ

5. **Tom and his brother counted the wheels on their toy cars. They counted 1,032 wheels. Which expression best shows how to find out how many cars the boys have?**

    Ⓐ (1000 + 30 + 2) - 4
    Ⓑ (1000 ÷ 4) + (32 ÷ 4)
    Ⓒ 258 + 258 + 258 + 258
    Ⓓ 1032 x 4

6.   The toothpick factory produces 423 toothpicks per hour. About how many toothpicks do they produce in 24 hours?

PART A

Which is the best equation to estimate how many toothpicks the factory produces in 24 hours?

Ⓐ 400 x 20 = 800
Ⓑ 425 x 25 = 10,625
Ⓒ 500 x 30 = 15,000

PART B

Show or explain why this is the best estimate.

7.   The measure of ∠DEF is 150°. The measure of ∠DEA is 130°.

Find the value of y.

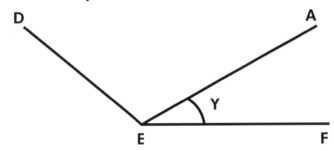

PART A

What is the value of y?

Write your answer in the box.

PART B

How do you know? Show or explain how you got your answer.

8. What is the sum of $\frac{4}{10} + \frac{48}{100}$?

    Ⓐ $\frac{88}{100}$

    Ⓑ $\frac{52}{100}$

    Ⓒ $\frac{9}{10}$

    Ⓓ $\frac{484}{1000}$

9. Enter your answer in the box.

    Calculate the product 462 x 3 = [   ]

10. Sara is making bows out of 1 yard strips of ribbon. For each bow, she needs a piece of yarn that is $\frac{1}{4}$ yard long. In order to use the template below, Sara must mark where $\frac{1}{4}$ and $\frac{3}{4}$ would be found on the number line. Complete the number line by labeling points at $\frac{1}{4}$ and $\frac{3}{4}$.

11. Maddy is saving up money to buy a bike. In March, she saved $32.00. In April, she saved three times as much money as she saved In March.

    PART A

    Write the numbers and symbols into the blanks to complete an equation that can be used to find a, how much money Maddy saved in April. Each number and symbol may be used more than once or not at all.

    Write the numbers and symbols into the correct order.

    | 32 | 3 | 2 | + | - | ÷ | x |

    [   ] [   ] [   ] = a

How much money did Maddy save in April?

Write your answer in the box. | $

12. Peg and Dan were making lists of equivalent fractions for their math homework.

Peg's list had the following fractions:

$\frac{1}{4}$, $\frac{2}{8}$, $\frac{3}{11}$

Dan's list had the following fractions:

$\frac{1}{3}$, $\frac{2}{6}$, $\frac{3}{9}$

PART A

Which child wrote a list of fractions that are all equivalent?
In the box, write the name of the child who used only equivalent fractions.

PART B

How do you know the list is only equivalent fractions? Explain how you know.

13. The Frank family bought a carton of milk. The first day they drank $\frac{2}{8}$ of the carton. The next day they drank $\frac{3}{8}$.

PART A

How much of the milk did they drink in all?

Write your answer as a fraction in the box.

      LumosLearning.com   ▲

PART B

After the two days, how much of the carton of milk was left?

Show or explain how you got your answer.

```


```

14. Which two of the following five numbers are composite?

 3   14   6   7   19

Write the two composite numbers into the boxes below.

```
            
```

15. What is the quotient of 300 ÷ 30?

PART A

Write your answer in the box. _____

PART B

How do you know? Show or explain how you got your answer.

```


```

16. Which two numbers below are multiples of 6?

Ⓐ 3
Ⓑ 12
Ⓒ 16
Ⓓ 26
Ⓔ 36

17. Write the correct comparison symbol (<, >, or =) in the box.

$$\frac{2}{3} \quad \boxed{} \quad \frac{3}{4}$$

End of Performance Based Assessment (PBA) - 1

Performance Based Assessment (PBA) - 1

Answer Key

Question No.	Answer	Related Lumos Online Workbook	CCSS
1 PART A	5 slices.	Multi-step Problems; Number Sentences; Real World Problems	4.OA.3-1
1 PART B	*	Multi-step Problems; Number Sentences; Real World Problems	4.OA.3-1
2	6,109	Addition & Subtraction	4.NBT.4
3	0.9	Convert Fractions to Decimals	4.NF.6
4	D	Points, Lines, Rays and Segments; Angle Measurement	4.G.1
5	B	Division	4.NBT.5
6 PART A	B	Rounding Numbers	4.NBT.3
6 PART B	*	Rounding Numbers	4.NBT.3
7 PART A	20°	Angle Measurement	4.MD.7
7 PART B	*	Angle Measurement	4.MD.7
8	A	Equivalent Fractions	4.NF.5
9	1,386	Division; Multiplication; Addition & Subtraction; Rounding Numbers; Compare Numbers and Expanded Notation; Place Value	4.NBT.5-1
10	*	Representing and Interpreting Data; Perimeter & Area; Measurement Problems; Units of Measurement	4.MD.4-1
11 PART A	$32 x 3 = a	Real World Problems	4.OA.2
11 PART B	$96	Real World Problems	4.OA.2
12 PART A	Dan	Equivalent Fractions; Compare Fractions	4.NF.1-2
12 PART B	*	Equivalent Fractions; Compare Fractions	4.NF.1-2
13 PART A	$\frac{5}{8}$	Adding & Subtracting Fractions	4.NF.3d

* See detailed explanation

 LumosLearning.com ▲

Question No.	Answer	Related Lumos Online Workbook	CCSS
13 PART B	*	Adding & Subtracting Fractions	4.NF.3d
14	6 and 14	Number Theory	4.OA.4-4
15 PART A	10	Place Value	4.NBT.1
15 PART B	*	Place Value	4.NBT.1
16	B and E	Number Theory; Multi-step Problems; Real World Problems	4.OA.4-2
17	<	Compare Fractions; Equivalent Fractions	4.NF.2-1

* See detailed explanation

Performance Based Assessment (PBA) - 1

Detailed Explanations

Question No.	Answer	Detailed Explanation
1 PART A	5 slices	This is a two-step word problem involving multiplication of whole numbers. In the first step, the total number of leftover slices of pizza is determined. As there are 4 identical pizzas and each is cut into 8 equal slices, the total number of slices (4 x 8) is 32. Since there are 27 students, the equation 32 – 27 is used to determine there are 5 leftover slices.
1 PART B		The second step requires mathematical reasoning. Though the wording may be slightly different and informal, a correct answer would indicate that the first step is to multiply 4 x 8 or use repeat addition (8 + 8 + 8 + 8) to determine there are 32 slices of pizza in all. Then, you must find the difference (use subtraction) between the total number of slices (32) and the number of students (27) using the equation 32-27, which equals 5 leftover slices.
2	6,109	This exercise involves subtracting two four-digit numbers. The difference between 7,402 and 1,293 equals 6,109 (7,402 - 1,293 = 6,109).
3	0.9	This exercise involves using decimal notation for a fraction with a denominator of 10. The fraction 9/10 is equivalent to the decimal 0.9, both of which are read as nine tenths. Because the denominator of 10 indicates tenths, there is one digit to the right of the decimal point to also indicate tenths. The box above 0.9 on the number line should be checked.
4	D	This exercise involves identifying a line segment. Since (a) is a ray, (b) is an acute angle and (c) is a pair of parallel lines, the answer is (d) because a line segment has two endpoints and each endpoint is often labeled with a corresponding letter.
5	B	This exercise requiring mathematical reasoning to determine the quotient of a four-digit number and a one-digit number based on strategies using place value. To find how many cars the boys have, 1,032 is divided by 4. Answer (b) $(1000 \div 4) + (32 \div 4)$ shows the division of 1,032 by decomposing the number into 1,000 and 32, both of which are divisible by 4.

LumosLearning.com   ▲

Question No.	Answer	Detailed Explanation
6 PART A	B	This is a two-step problem requiring the use of place value to round multi-digit numbers to make an estimate. In the first step, the number of bouncy balls produced per hour (423) and the time period of 24 hours must both be rounded to provide an equation that allows for the best estimate. Rounding 423 to 425 and rounding 24 to 25 provides the best estimate, so answer (b) 425 x 25 = 10,625 is correct.
6 PART B		The second step requires mathematical reasoning. Though the wording may be slightly different and informal, a correct answer would mention rounding each number to a compatible number. (425 and 25 are compatible numbers.)
7 PART A	20°	This is a two-step problem requiring recognizing of angles as additive. In the first step, the equation value of y is required. Because $\angle$ DEF is 150° and $\angle$DEA is 130°, the value of y can be found using the equation 150° - 130° = y, giving the value of y as 20°
7 PART B		The second step requires mathematical reasoning. Though the wording may be slightly different and informal, a correct answer would include the subtraction equation 150° - 130° = 20° or the addition equation 130° + 20° = 150°, both of which show an understanding that angles are additive.
8	A	This exercise requires expressing a fraction with a denominator of 10 as an equivalent fraction with a denominator of 100, and then the addition of the two fractions with like denominators of 100. First, the fraction 4/10 is multiplied by 10/10 so that the denominator is 100, or 4/10 x 10/10 = 40/100. Now, 40/100 + 48/100 can be added. The sum is (a) 88/100, which is an example of the addition of fractions with like denominators.
9	1,386	This exercise is the multiplication of a three-digit number and a one-digit number. The product of 462 x 3 is 1,386.
10		This exercise involves using a number line to display a set of measurements in 1/4 fractions of a unit. The fractions 1/4 and 3/4 which represent the segments of yarn length Sara needs to make bows are to be placed on the number line. The correct placement for ¼ is halfway between 0 and ½ and for ¾ is halfway between ½ and 1 as shown below:

```
        0         1/4         1/2         3/4          1

        |----------|-----------|-----------|-----------|
```

Question No.	Answer	Detailed Explanation
11 PART A	$32 x 3 = a	This is a two part question that requires representing a verbal statement of a multiplicative comparison as an equation. If Maddy saved three times as much money in April as in March (which was $32), then the equation that represents how much money Maddy saved in April is $32 x 3 = a.
11 PART B	$96	The second step is to solve for a by multiplying 32 x 3. The result is $96.
12 PART A	Dan	This is a two-part question requiring the use of the formula a/b= (n x a)/(n x b) to find equivalent fractions. Two lists are presented. The solution is to determine which child's list contains all equivalent fractions. Dan's list contains only equivalent fractions because: 1/3 x 2/2 = 2/6 and 1/3 x 3/3= 3/9. Peg's list contains only two equivalent fractions, 1/4 , 2/8 because 1/4 x 2/2 = 2/8. 3/11 is not an equivalent fraction to 1/4 or 2/8.
12 PART B		The second step requires mathematical reasoning. Though the wording may be slightly different and informal, a correct answer would include using the formula a/b = (n x a)/(n x b) to show 1/3 x 2/2 = 2/6 and 1/3 x 3/3 = 3/9. And, to explain that 1/4 x 3/3 ≠ 3/11.
13 PART A	$\frac{5}{8}$	This is a two part question to solve a word problem involving the addition and subtraction of fractions with like denominators. In the first step, the amount of milk the Frank family drank in two days is added together using the equation 2/8+ 3/8, which results in 5/8..
13 PART B		The second step is to determine how much of the milk was left, which is 3/8 . This requires mathematical reasoning. Though the wording may be slightly different and informal, a correct answer would include the equations 8/8 - 5/8 = 3/8 or 5/8+ 3/8 = 8/8 or one whole. It would be acceptable if these equations were represented pictorially.
14	6 and 14	This exercise involves determining whether a given whole number is a composite. Of the five numbers presented (3, 14, 6, 7, and 19) the two composite numbers are 6 and 14. That is because they both have other factors besides one and themselves.

LumosLearning.com   ▲

Question No.	Answer	Detailed Explanation
15 PART A	10	This is a two-part question involving the recognition in a multi-digit whole number that a digit in one place represents ten times what it represents in the place to its right. To find the quotient of the application of concepts of place value and division are needed. $300 \div 30 = 10$
15 PART B		The second step requires the demonstration of mathematical reasoning. Though the wording may be slightly different and informal, a correct answer would indicate the use of multiplication to solve the division problem: $30 \times 10 = 300$. And/or to the explanation that explains a digit in one place represents ten times what it represents in the place to its right. And/or the explanation that 30 goes into 300, 10 times and to show that with the use of repeat addition.
16	B and E	This is an exercise involving multiples. The two numbers that are multiples of 6 are (b) 12 and (e) 36.
17	<	This exercise is the comparison of fractions with unlike denominators. As 2/3 is less than 3/4, the less than sign (<) is correct: 2/3 < 3/4 That is because making the two fractions into equivalent fractions with like denominators results in: $2/3 \times 4/4 = 8/12$ and $3/4 \times 3/3 = 9/12$ and $8/12 < 9/12$

Notes

     LumosLearning.com   ▲

Performance Based Assessment (PBA) - 2

Student Name:
Test Date:

Start Time:
End Time:

> **Here are some reminders for when you are taking the Grade 4 Mathematics Performance Based Assessment (PBA).**
>
> To answer the questions on the test, use the directions given in the question. If you do not know the answer to a question, skip it and go on to the next question. If time permits, you may return to questions in this session only. Do your best to answer every question.

1. Mrs. Patel wanted to bake a cake with the largest area. She had three baking pans to choose from:

   • Pan A was 3 cm. long and 8 cm. wide
   • Pan B was 7 cm. long and 4 cm. wide
   • Pan C was 5 cm. long and 5 cm. wide

   PART A

   What is the area of each baking pan? Enter your answer in the boxes.

   Pan A [＿＿＿＿＿＿] sq. cm.

   Pan B [＿＿＿＿＿＿] sq. cm.

   Pan C [＿＿＿＿＿＿] sq. cm.

   PART B

   Which pan should she use to bake a cake with the largest area?

   Enter your answer in the box. [＿＿＿＿＿＿]

How do you know which rectangle has the largest area?

Show or explain how you got your answer.

2. Enter your answer in the box.

    Calculate the sum. 1054 + 6537=

3. Draw the angle that corresponds with the words below.

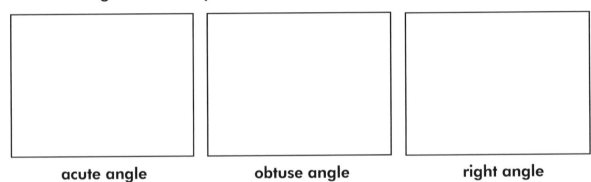

        acute angle   obtuse angle   right angle

4. Find the difference between the fractions $\frac{4}{6}$ and $\frac{3}{6}$.

    Enter your answer as a fraction in the box. $\frac{4}{6}$ - $\frac{3}{6}$ =

5. Write the correct comparison symbol (<, >, or =) in the box.

    $2\frac{4}{5}$ ☐ $1+1+\frac{1}{5}+\frac{1}{5}$

6. Maya was finding factor pairs for the number 40. Maya's list of factor pairs for 40 is below:

1 and 40
2 and 20
4 and 10
5 and 8

                    ▼

How can Maya best explain that her answers are correct?

Ⓐ When you add the factor pairs together then divide by 40, the result is an even number.
Ⓑ The difference between the number pairs is 40.
Ⓒ When you multiply the two numbers in each factor pair, the product is 40.
Ⓓ When you subtract the two numbers in each factor pair then divide by the first number, the result is 40.

7.   How many centimeters are there in 3 meters?

Ⓐ 30
Ⓑ 100
Ⓒ 300
Ⓓ 3000

8.   The rule for the number pattern below is "Add 5".

5, 10, 15, 20...

PART A

What is the next number in the pattern?

Enter your answer in the box. [   ]

PART B

What do you notice about the numbers in the pattern? Explain why the numbers will continue in this way.

[   ]

9.   Enter your answer in the box.

Calculate the quotient. 6415 ÷ 5 = [   ]

10. **The Singh family wants to take a car trip from Baltimore to New York City. The total distance is 180 miles. If they can drive 60 miles in one hour and make no stops, how long will the trip take?**

PART A

How many hours will it take them to go from Baltimore to New York?

Enter your answer in the box.
┌─────────────────────┐
│   │
└─────────────────────┘

PART B

Complete the conversion table to identify how many minutes it will take them to travel from Baltimore to New York City by car.

hours	minutes
1	
	120
3	
	240

It will take the Singh family _____ minutes to travel from Baltimore to New York City by car.

11. Which expression best shows how to solve 52 x 18?

Ⓐ (50 x 2) x (10 x 8)
Ⓑ 16 + 400 + 20 + 500
Ⓒ 52 + 52 + 18 + 18
Ⓓ 468 + 468

12. What fraction is equivalent to the decimal .37?

Write your answer in the box.
┌─────────────────────┐
│   │
└─────────────────────┘

13. The Carlson family is serving a turkey dinner for 5 people. If each person at the dinner party will eat $\frac{3}{4}$ of a pound of turkey, how many pounds of turkey will be needed?

PART A

Shade $\frac{1}{4}$ fraction pieces into each of the whole circles shown below to best show how many pounds of turkey will be needed to feed 5 people $\frac{3}{4}$ of a pound of turkey each.

Some or all of the $\frac{1}{4}$ fraction pieces and whole circles can be used.

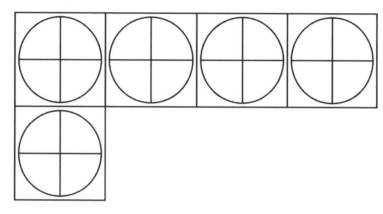

PART B

How many pounds of turkey is needed? Show or explain how you got your answer.

PART C

Between what two whole numbers does your answer lie?

My answer is between _____ and _____.

14. The ruler shown below measures in centimeters. What is the length of the snake drawing, including its tongue, to the nearest cm?

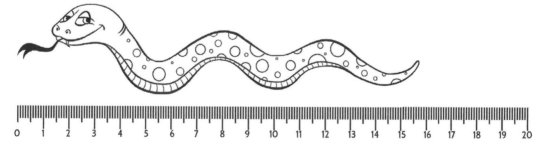

Write you answer as a decimal in the box.

15. Lola was training for her next track meet. She ran around the track 8 times. If each lap around the track is $\frac{1}{4}$ mile, how far did Lola run in all?

Ⓐ 1 mile
Ⓑ $1\frac{1}{2}$ miles
Ⓒ 2 miles
Ⓓ $2\frac{1}{4}$ miles

16. On Saturday, 6,918 people attended the Clark County Fair. 8,732 people attended the fair on Sunday. How many more people attended on Sunday than on Saturday?

Enter your answer in the box. [   ] people

17. Round 235,602 to the nearest thousand.

PART A

Which number best shows 245,602 rounded to the nearest thousand?

Ⓐ 200,000
Ⓑ 245,600
Ⓒ 245,000
Ⓓ 246,000

PART B

Which digit in 235,602 is in the thousands place?

Enter your answer in the box. [   ]

End of Performance Based Assessment (PBA) - 2

     LumosLearning.com   ▼

Performance Based Assessment (PBA) - 2

Answer Key

Question No.	Answer	Related Lumos Online Workbook	CCSS
1 PART A	24, 28 and 25 sq. cm.	Perimeter & Area	4.MD.3
1 PART B	B	Perimeter & Area	4.MD.3
1 Part C	*	Perimeter & Area	4.MD.3
2	7,591	Addition & Subtraction; Rounding Numbers; Compare Numbers and Expanded Notation; Place Value	4.NBT.4-1
3	*	Angles	4.G.2
4	$\frac{1}{6}$	Adding & Subtracting Fractions	4.NF.3a
5	>	Adding & Subtracting Fractions	4.NF.3b-1
6	C	Number Theory; Multi-step Problems; Real World Problems; Number Sentences	4.OA.4-1
7	C	Units of Measurement	4.MD.1
8 PART A	25	Patterns	4.OA.5
8 PART B	*	Patterns	4.OA.5
9	1,283	Division	4.NBT.6-2
10 PART A	3 hours	Measurement Problems; Units of Measurement	4.MD.2-1
10 PART B	*	Measurement Problems; Units of Measurement	4.MD.2-1
11	B	Division; Multiplication; Addition & Subtraction; Compare Numbers and Expanded Notation; Rounding Numbers	4.NBT.5-2
12	$\frac{37}{100}$	Convert Fractions to Decimals	4.NF.6
13 PART A	*	Multiplying Fractions	4.NF.4c

* See detailed explanation

Question No.	Answer	Related Lumos Online Workbook	CCSS
13 PART B	3 3/4	Multiplying Fractions	4.NF.4c
13 Part C	*	Multiplying Fractions	4.NF.4c
14	.16 cm	Units of Measurement	4.MD.1
15 PART A	C	Measurement Problems	4.MD.2-2
16	1,814	Multi-step Problems	4.OA.3
17 PART A	D	Rounding Numbers	4.NBT.3
17 PART B	5	Place Value	4.NBT.1

* See detailed explanation

           LumosLearning.com   ▼

Performance Based Assessment (PBA) - 2

Detailed Explanations

Question No.	Answer	Detailed Explanation
1 PART A	24, 28 and 25 sq. cm.	This is a three-part question involving the application of the formula for determine and comparing the areas (a = l x w) of three different cake pans. In the first step, the area of each baking pan is calculated using the formula. Pan A (3 cm by 8 cm) = 24 sq. cm Pan B (7 cm by 4 cm) = 28 sq. cm Pan C (5 cm by 5 cm) = 25 sq. cm
1 PART B		The second step is to determine which baking pan has the largest area. Pan B has the largest area (28 sq. cm) compared to Pan A (24 sq. cm) and Pan C (25 sq. cm).
1 Part C		The third step requires mathematical reasoning. Though the wording may be slightly different and informal, a correct answer would include using the formula for area (a=lxw). For example, for Pan A, 3x8=24; Pan B, 7x4=28 and Pan C, 5x5= 25. A diagram is also acceptable which shows the dimensions of each pan.
2	7,591	This exercise involves the addition of two four-digit numbers. The sum of 1,054+ 6,537 is 7,591.
3		This exercise involves drawing (creating) right, acute and obtuse angles. A ray is provided and one of the sides is to be manipulated to create each angle. For the acute, any angle less than 90° and greater than 0° is correct, such as: Acute Angle For the obtuse, any angle greater than 90° and less than 180° is correct, such as: Obtuse Angle For the right angle, only an angle that equals 90° is correct: Right Angle

Question No.	Answer	Detailed Explanation
4	$\dfrac{1}{6}$	This exercise involves subtracting fractions with like denominators. 4/6 - 3/6 = 1/6. That is because fractions with like denominators can be subtracted from each other.
5	>	This exercise requires understanding the decomposition of a fraction. It requires comparing a mixed number to a fraction number sentence. For example, 1 + 1+ 1/5 + 1/5 results in 2 2/5, and the correct comparison symbol is greater than (>); 2 4/5 > 1 + 1+ 1/5 + 1/5
6	C	This exercise involves using mathematical reasoning behind finding factoring pairs for a whole number in the range 1-100. Because factor pairs are two numbers that, when multiplied together, equal another number, (or product,) then the (c) "When you multiply the two numbers in each factor pair, the product is 40." is the best answer, because 1 x 40 = 40; 2 x 20 = 40; 5 x 8 = 40, and 4 x 10 = 40.
7	C	This exercise involves knowing the measurement of units within a system (cm to m). Because there are 100 cm in each meter, then there are (c) 300 cm in 3 meters.
8 Part A	25	To identify the next number in the pattern 5, 10, 15, 20 with the rule "Add 5". The next number in the pattern is 25.
8 Part B		This is a two-step problem that involves generating a number pattern that follows a given rule. The first step is to identify the next number in the pattern 5, 10, 15, 20 with the rule "Add 5". The next number in the pattern is 25. The second step requires the mathematical reasoning to determine what can be noticed about the numbers in the pattern. Though the wording may be different and informal, a correct answer would indicate that there is a pattern between the one and tens place. The ones place pattern alternates between 0 and 5. The tens place pattern has two numbers with one in the tens place, then two numbers with a two in the tens place.
9	1,283	This exercise involves finding a whole-number quotient with a four-digit dividend and one-digit divisor. The quotient of 6,415 ÷ 5 is 1,283.
10 PART A	3 hours	This is a two-step question involving division to solve a word problem about distance. In the first step, the time it would take to drive between Baltimore and New York City (180 miles) at 60 miles per hour must be calculated. The equation to solve this is 180 miles ÷ 60 miles per hour = 3 hours.

          LumosLearning.com   ▼

Question No.	Answer	Detailed Explanation
10 PART B		The second step requires expressing measurements given in a larger term (hours) as a smaller unit (minutes). To solve this, fill in the conversion table as shown below, the correct answers are in bold:

hours	minutes
1	**60**
2	120
3	**180**
4	240

It will take the Singh family 180 minutes to travel from Baltimore to New York City by car.

Question No.	Answer	Detailed Explanation
11	B	This exercise mathematical reasoning based on understanding place values to solve a two-digit by two-digit multiplication problem. The equation which best represents how to solve 52 x 18 is (b) 16 + 400 + 20 + 500. That is because it shows the product of multiplying 52 x 8 as 2 x 8 = 16 and 50 x 8 = 400, then 52 x 10 as 2 x 10 = 20 an 50 x 10 = 500. The sum of all the parts 16 + 400 + 20 + 500 is 936, which is the same result as using the algorithm to solve 52 x 18.
12	$\frac{37}{100}$	This exercise involves rewriting a decimal as a fraction equivalent. The fraction equivalent of the decimal 0.37 is 37/100. That is because the decimal is two digits to the right of the decimal point indicating the place value is in the hundredths. The decimal, therefore, is representing thirty-seven hundredths, so the fraction's denominator would then be 100 and the numerator 37.
13 PART A, B & C		This exercise is a three-step word problem involving multiplying a fraction by a whole number using fraction model to represent the problem. In the first step, 1/4 fraction pieces are placed into the whole circles to show how many pounds of turkey will be needed to feed 5 people, 3/4 of a pound of turkey each. This requires 15 1/4 fraction pieces, because 5 x 3/4 = 15 x 1/4. This results in covering 3 3/4 whole circles. The second step requires mathematical reasoning. Though the wording may be different, a correct answer would indicate that they used 15 1/4 fraction pieces, or used 3 1/4 fraction pieces 5 times to get the result of 3 3/4 . The third step requires selecting the two whole numbers between which 3 3/4 lies, which are 3 and 4.
14	.16 cm	This exercise involves measuring to the nearest cm on a number line using decimal notation. The snake drawing is about .16 cm in length.

Question No.	Answer	Detailed Explanation
15	C	This exercise is a word problem involving distance and the multiplication of a whole number and a unit fraction. The equations to solve are: 8 x 1/4 = 8/4 = 2 or 1/4 + 1/4 +1/4 + 1/4 + 1/4 + 1/4 + 1/4 + 1/4 =8/4 = 2 The answer is (c) 2 miles.
16	1,814	This is a one-step word problem involving subtracting two four-digit numbers. The difference between the number of people who attend the country fair on Saturday (6,918) and Sunday (8,732) is 1,814 people.
17 PART A	D	In the second step, the number rounded to the nearest thousand is D 246,000.
17 PART B	5	This is a two-step problem involving the rounding of a multi-digit number to the thousands place. In the first step, the thousands digit in the number 245,602 is identified. The digit in the thousands place is 5.

Notes

End-Of-Year Assessment (EOY) - 1

Student Name: **Start Time:**

Test Date: **End Time:**

Here are some reminders for when you are taking the Grade 4 Mathematics End-of-Year Assessment (EOY).

To answer the questions on the test, use the directions given in the question. If you do not know the answer to a question, skip it and go on to the next question. If time permits, you may return to questions in this session only. Do your best to answer every question.

---

1. **Which equation represents "42 is 6 times as many as 7"?**

    Ⓐ $42 = 6 + 7$
    Ⓑ $42 = 7 + 6$
    Ⓒ $42 = 6 \times 7$
    Ⓓ $42 = 6 \times 8$

2. **Mateo made brownies in a rectangular pan. He cut the brownies into 8 equal pieces. He then gave 3 pieces to his brother and 2 pieces to his friend.**

    PART A

    What fraction of the whole brownie did Mateo give away in all?

    Enter you answer as a fraction in the box. _____

PART B

Which two of these expressions could represent the fraction of the brownie that Mateo gave away in all?

Ⓐ $\frac{1}{8}+\frac{1}{8}+\frac{1}{8}+\frac{1}{8}+\frac{1}{8}+\frac{1}{8}+\frac{1}{8}+\frac{1}{8}$

Ⓑ $\frac{3}{8}+\frac{2}{8}$

Ⓒ $3+2$

Ⓓ $\frac{1}{8}+5$

Ⓔ $\frac{1}{8}+\frac{1}{8}+\frac{1}{8}+\frac{1}{8}+\frac{1}{8}$

3. Select the three choices that are factor pairs for the number 12.

Ⓐ 1 and 12
Ⓑ 2 and 6
Ⓒ 3 and 5
Ⓓ 4 and 3
Ⓔ 5 and 7
Ⓕ 7 and 5

4. Enter your answer in the box.

Find the sum. 4739 + 2568 = [   ]

5. Which expression is equivalent to $5 \times \frac{3}{4}$?

Ⓐ $1 \times \frac{8}{4}$

Ⓑ $5 \times \frac{1}{4}$

Ⓒ $10 \times \frac{3}{4}$

Ⓓ $15 \times \frac{1}{4}$

6. The whiteboard in Mrs. Crosby's classroom has a total area of 36 sq. ft. If the whiteboard is 9 feet long, how wide is the whiteboard?

    (A) 4 ft.
    (B) 5 ft.
    (C) 6 ft.
    (D) 405 ft.

7. Richi has 36 quarters. He wants to buy a used video game that costs $8.

    PART A

    How many dollars does 36 quarters equal?

    Enter your answer in the box. [   ] dollar(s)

    PART B

    If Richi buys the used video game for $8, how much money will he have left?

    Enter your answer in the box. [   ] dollar(s)

8. Write the correct comparison symbol (<, >, or =) in the box.

    2, 356 [   ] 2000 + 500 + 30 + 1

9. Enter your answer in the box.

    Find the product. 631 x 6 = [   ]

10. Marque made a wooden picture frame that was 24 inches long and 12 inches wide. He cut a ½" wide wooden board to make the frame.

    PART A

    What was the perimeter of the frame?

    Enter your answer in the box. [   ] inches

The hardware store only sells wood by the foot. How many feet of board did Marque need to make the picture frame?

PART B

Enter your answer in the box.

	feet

PART C

Complete the conversion table to show how many feet long the board was.

inches	feet
_____	1
24	_____
36	3
_____	4
60	5
_____	_____

11. $\frac{32}{100}$ is equivalent to which of the following decimals?

Ⓐ 32.00
Ⓑ 3.2
Ⓒ 0.32
Ⓓ 100.32

12. Which two of the following numbers are composite?

5, 13, 37, 45, 71, 88

Ⓐ 5
Ⓑ 13
Ⓒ 37
Ⓓ 45
Ⓔ 71
Ⓕ 88

13. Make this equation true. Enter your answer in the box.

$$\frac{2}{10} + \frac{18}{100} = \frac{\boxed{}}{100}$$

14. Max and Rodney both got the same sized candy bar. Max ate 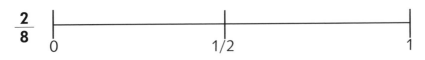 $\frac{2}{8}$ of his candy bar. Rodney ate $\frac{3}{4}$ of his candy bar.

PART A

Place the dot to show where each fraction belongs on the number line:

$\frac{2}{8}$

$\frac{3}{4}$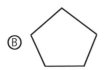

PART B

Did Max or Rodney eat more of his candy bar? Enter your answer in the box.

[   ] ate more of his candy bar.

15. Enter your answer in the box.

    Find the product. 23 x 18 = [   ]

16. Which two figures have at least one pair of parallel lines?

    Ⓐ

    Ⓑ

    Ⓒ

    Ⓓ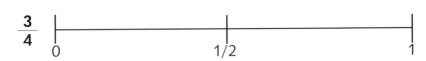

    Ⓔ

17. At a bake sale, Tia and Jaden earned $147 from the cookies they had sold. Then they paid Tia's mother back $18 for materials to make the cookies.

PART A

After the children paid Tia's mother back for materials, how much did they earn at the bake sale.

Enter your answer in the box. | $ |

PART B

If the two children split their earnings equally, how much would each child get?

Enter your answer in the box. | $ |

18. Mr. Rhode's class collected pennies for the penny drive to give to a local charity. They collected pennies for five days as shown in the table below.

Monday	112
Tuesday	53
Wednesday	205
Thursday	189
Friday	226

PART A

How many pennies did Mr. Rhode's class collect in all?

Enter your answer in the box. | | pennies

PART B

Round the total number of pennies they collected to the nearest hundred.

Enter your answer in the box. | | pennies

19. Compare the decimals 0.46 and 0.13

    Write the correct comparison symbol (<, >, or =) in the box.

    0.46 ⬚ 0.13

20. Which set of numbers are all multiples of 3?

    Ⓐ 1, 6, 14
    Ⓑ 3, 9, 16
    Ⓒ 6, 9, 12
    Ⓓ 5, 6, 9

21. Write the correct comparison symbol (<, >, or =) in the box.

    $\dfrac{1}{4}$ ⬚ $\dfrac{5}{8}$

22. Which angle has a measure closest to 35°?

    You can use the protractor to help you find the answer.

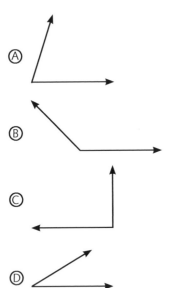

Ⓐ

Ⓑ

Ⓒ

Ⓓ

          LumosLearning.com   ◀

23. Enter your answer in the box.

Find the quotient. 1825 ÷ 5 = ⬚

24. Which two figures are showing a line of symmetry?

Ⓐ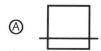

Ⓑ

Ⓒ

Ⓓ

Ⓔ

25. The 4th graders at Sunny Hills Elementary are going on a field trip to the state capital. It takes 15 minutes to get all the children from their classroom and loaded onto the bus. It takes at least 1 hours and 15 minutes for the bus to drive from Sunny Hills Elementary to the state capital.

PART A

What is the minimum time, in minutes will it take for the 4th graders to get from their classroom, loaded on to the bus, and driven to the state capital?

It will take at least _____ minutes.

PART B

Assuming the drive can be completed in the time allowed, what is the latest possible time the 4th graders need to leave their classroom for the field trip if they need to arrive no later than 10:30 A.M.?

Enter your answer in the box. ⬚

26. JoJo's Sand-wich shop made 1,432 sub sandwiches in March and 2,591 sub sandwiches in April. How many more sandwiches did they make in April than in March?

Enter your answer in the box. [   ] sub sandwiches

27. The rule for the input/output table below is "Multiply by 3". Complete the table by entering a number in each box which best follows the rule.

IN	1	2	7		12	
OUT	3	6		30	36	45

28. Add $2\frac{1}{3} + 1\frac{1}{3}$

Ⓐ $3\frac{1}{3}$

Ⓑ $3\frac{1}{6}$

Ⓒ $3\frac{2}{6}$

Ⓓ $3\frac{2}{3}$

29. How many ounces (oz.) are in 4 pounds (lb.)? Complete the conversion table to solve.

OZ.	lb.
___	1
32	___
48	3
___	4

30. Eva is throwing a party. She figures that each guest will eat $\frac{3}{8}$ of a pizza. There are 7 people, including herself, at the party.

PART A

How much pizza does Eva need to feed 7 people if they each eat $\frac{3}{8}$ of a pizza each?

Enter your answer in the box as a mixed number.

$$7 \times \frac{3}{8} = \boxed{}$$

PART B

How many whole pizzas will she need to buy?

Enter your answer in the box. $\boxed{}$ pizzas

31. On Tuesday, the baker made 36 dozen cupcakes. Since a dozen equals 12, how many cupcakes were baked in all on Tuesday?

Enter your answer in the box. $\boxed{}$ cupcakes

32. Which fraction model best shows $\frac{2}{5} + \frac{3}{5}$?

Ⓐ

Ⓑ

Ⓒ

Ⓓ

33. Which set of fractions are all equivalent to $\frac{1}{4}$?

Ⓐ $\frac{2}{8}, \frac{3}{8}, \frac{4}{16}$

Ⓑ $\frac{1}{8}, \frac{1}{12}, \frac{1}{16}$

Ⓒ $\frac{2}{8}, \frac{3}{12}, \frac{4}{16}$

Ⓓ $\frac{1}{2}, \frac{2}{4}, \frac{4}{4}$

34. The Nuts O' Lot peanut factory packaged 1,265 cans of peanuts on Monday, 2,019 on Tuesday and 1,932 on Wednesday. How many cans of peanuts were packaged in all during the three day period?

Ⓐ 4,106
Ⓑ 5,126
Ⓒ 5,216
Ⓓ 6,215

35. Use the numbers below that best solve the division problem.

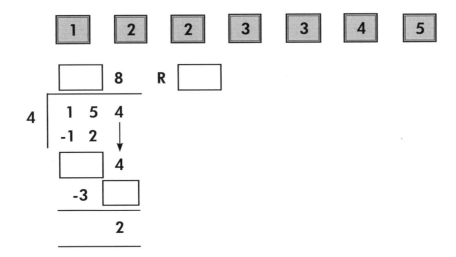

36. Which two expressions are equal to $\dfrac{5}{6}$?

Ⓐ $\dfrac{1}{6} + \dfrac{1}{6} + \dfrac{1}{6} + \dfrac{1}{6} + \dfrac{1}{6}$

Ⓑ $\dfrac{1}{6} + \dfrac{2}{6} + \dfrac{3}{6} + \dfrac{4}{6} + \dfrac{5}{6}$

Ⓒ $\dfrac{6}{6} - \dfrac{2}{6}$

Ⓓ $\dfrac{1}{6} + \dfrac{2}{6} + \dfrac{1}{6} + \dfrac{1}{6}$

Ⓔ $1 + \dfrac{5}{6}$

37. Place a dot at 0.76 on the number line.

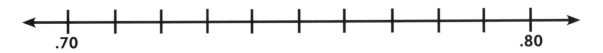

.70   .80

38. A circle measures 360°. If a circle was broken into 6 equal parts, what is the measure of each interior angle?

Enter your answer in the box. [   ]

39. Which two figures each have at least one acute interior angle?

Ⓐ

Ⓑ

Ⓒ

Ⓓ

Ⓔ

End of End-Of-Year Assessment (EOY) - 1

End-Of-Year Assessment (EOY) -1
Answer Key

Question No.	Answer	Related Lumos Online Workbook	CCSS
1	C	Number Sentences	4.OA.1.1
2 PART A	$\frac{5}{8}$	Adding & Subtracting Fractions	4.NF.3a
2 PART B	B	Adding & Subtracting Fractions	4.NF.3d
3	A, B, D	Number Theory	4.OA.4
4	7,307	Addition & Subtraction	4.NBT.4
5	D	Multiplying Fractions	4.NF.4a
6	A	Perimeter & Area	4.MD.3
7 PART A	$9	Multi-step Problems; Real World Problems; Number Sentences	4.OA.3-1
7 PART B	$1	Multi-step Problems; Real World Problems; Number Sentences	4.OA.3-1
8	<	Compare Numbers and Expanded Notation	4.NBT.2
9	3,786	Division; Multiplication; Addition & Subtraction; Rounding Numbers; Compare Numbers and Expanded Notation; Place Value	4.NBT.5-1
10 PART A	72 inches	Perimeter & Area	4.MD.3
10 PART B	6 feet	Units of Measurement	4.MD.1
10 PART C	*	Units of Measurement	4.MD.1
11	C	Convert Fractions to Decimals	4.NF.6
12	D, F	Number Theory	4.OA.4-4
13	38	Equivalent Fractions	4.NF.1
14 PART A	*	Representing and Interpreting Data; Perimeter & Area; Measurement Problems; Units of Measurement	4.MD.4-1
14 PART B	Rodney	Measurement Problems	4.MD.2.2
15	414	Division; Multiplication; Addition & Subtraction; Compare Numbers and Expanded Notation; Rounding Numbers	4.NBT.5-2
16	A, D	Classifying Plance (2-D) Shapes; Points, Lines, Rays, and Segments	4.G.1
17 PART A	$129	Multi-step Problems; Real World Problems	4.OA.3.2

* See detailed explanation

Question No.	Answer	Related Lumos Online Workbook	CCSS
17 PART B	$64.50	Multi-step Problems; Real World Problems	4.OA.3.2
18 PART A	785	Addition & Subtraction	4.NBT.4
18 PART B	800	Rounding Numbers	4.NBT.3
19	>	Compare Decimals	4.NF.7
20	C	Number Theory	4.OA.4
21	<	Compare Fractions; Equivalent Fractions	4.NF.2-1
22	D	Angle Measurement	4.MD.6
23	365	Division	4.NBT.5
24	B and E	Symmetry	4.G.3
25 PART A	90 min	Units of Measurement	4.MD.1
25 PART B	9:00 am	Measurement Problems; Units of Measurement	4.MD.2-1
26	1,159	Addition & Subtraction	4.NBT.4
27	*	Patterns	4.OA.5
28	D	Adding & Subtracting Fractions	4.NF.3c
29	*	Units of Measurement	4.MD.1
30 PART A	$2\frac{5}{8}$	Multiplying Fractions	4.NF.4c
30 PART B	3	Multiplying Fractions	4.NF.4c
31	432	Multiplication	4.NBT.5
32	B	Adding & Subtracting Fractions	4.NF.3a
33	C	Equivalent Fractions; Compare Fractions	4.NF.1-2
34	C	Multi-step Problems	4.OA.3
35	*	Division; Multiplication; Addition & Subtraction; Rounding Numbers; Compare Numbers and Expanded Notation; Place Value	4.NBT.6-1
36	A and D	Adding & Subtracting Fractions; Compare Fractions; Equivalent Fractions	4.NF.3b-1
37	*	Convert Fractions to Decimals	4.NF.6
38	60°	Division	4.NBT.5
39	A and D	Angles	4.G.2

* See detailed explanation

End-Of-Year Assessment (EOY) -1

Detailed Explanations

Question No.	Answer	Detailed Explanation
1	C	This exercise requires an interpretation of the statement "42 is 6 times as many as 7" that most closely correlates to an equation. The equation $42 = 6 \times 7$ is the correct answer.
2 PART A	$\dfrac{5}{8}$	This is a two part question involving the addition and decomposition of fractions. The first step is to determine how to represent that 3 of the 8 pieces of the brownie AND 2 of the 8 pieces of brownie are given away. The fraction that represents this scenario is 5/8.
2 PART B	B	The second step is to decompose the fraction into the sum of fractions in more than one way. This can be done using the expressions (b) 3/8+2/8 and (e) 1/8 + 1/8 + 1/8+1/8 +1/8
3	A, B, D	This is a factoring exercise that requires three correct responses. The three factor pairs for 12 are (a) 1 and 12, (b) 2 and 6 and (d) 4 and 3 because each factor pair, when multiplied, equals twelve.
4	7,307	This exercise is the simple addition of two four-digit numbers. The sum is 7,307.
5	D	This is the multiplication of a whole number and a fraction. The product is 15/4 which is the same as 15 x 1/4.
6	A	This is an area problem in which the area (36 sq. ft.) and the length (9 ft.) are given. Two equations can be used to solve, $36 \div 9 = ?$ or $9 \times ? = 36$. The width of the whiteboard is 4 ft.
7 PART A	$9	This is a two-step question involving converting quarters into dollars and finding the difference between the amount of money possessed and the cost of a video game. The first step is to convert 36 quarters to dollars using a ratio of 4 to 1 ($4 \times ? = 36$. The answer is $9.
7 :PART B	$1	The second step is to find how much money is left. This requires the subtraction equation, $9-$8=$1. Richi has $1 left.
8	<	This exercise is a comparison of a four-digit number in standard form and expanded form. The expanded form of 2,000 + 500 + 30 + 1 should be converted to 2,531. Since 2,356 is less than 2,531, the less than symbol (<) is correct: 2,356 < 2,000 + 500 + 30 + 1

LumosLearning.com   ◄

Question No.	Answer	Detailed Explanation
9	3,786	The product of 631 x 6 is 3,786. Any method can be used to solve.
10 PART A	72 inches	This is a two-step exercise involving perimeter and conversion from inches to feet. The first step is to determine the perimeter of the picture from the dimensions of 24 inches long and 12 inches wide: 24 + 12 + 24 + 12 = 72 inches.
10 PART B	6 feet	
10 PART C	6 feet	The second step is to convert inches to feet by filling in the conversion table:

inches	feet
12	1
24	**2**
36	3
48	4
60	5
72	**6**

The length of the board is 6 feet.

Question No.	Answer	Detailed Explanation
11	C	This exercise is to use decimal notation for fractions with a denominator of 100. The decimal equivalent of 32/100 is 0.32
12	D and F	A composite number is a whole number that can be divided evenly by numbers other than 1 and itself (not prime numbers). 45 can be divided by 1, 3, 5, 9, 15, and 45. 88 can be divided by 1, 2, 4, 8, 11, 22, 44, and 88.
13	38	This exercise is adding fractions with denominators of 10 and 100 by finding equivalent fractions. The equivalent fraction with a denominator of 100 for 2/10 is 20/100. So, 20/100+ 18/100= 38/100. The numerator is to be entered. The correct numerator is 38.
14 PART A		This is a two-step exercise involving comparing fractions. The first step is to place a marker on the number line that corresponds with the given fraction using ½ as a benchmark

$$\frac{2}{8}$$

$$\frac{3}{4}$$

Question No.	Answer	Detailed Explanation
14 PART B		The second step is to compare 2/8 and ¾ to determine who ate more of his candy bar. Rodney ate more of his candy bar as ¾ is greater than 2/8.

Question No.	Answer	Detailed Explanation
15	414	The product of 23 x 18 = 414. Any method can be used to solve
16	A and D	This exercise is to classify two-dimensional figures based on the presence of parallel lines. Only the rectangle and the trapezoid have at least one set of parallel lines.
17 PART A	$129	This is a two-step exercise involving the division of whole numbers in which a remainder must be interpreted. The first step is to find the difference between what was earned ($147) and what was owed ($18), $147-$18= $129.
17 PART B	$64.50	The second step is to divide the remainder ($129) between the two children. Since $129 is not evenly divisible by 2, each child gets $64 with a remainder of $1. The remainder of $1 would then be split evenly to give each child an additional $.50. Each child gets $64.50.
18 PART A	785	This is a two-step exercise requiring computation to find the sum of several numbers, understanding of place value and rounding. In the first step, the sum of 5 days' worth of penny collecting must be found, 112 + 53 + 205 + 109 + 226 = 785.
18 PART B	800	The second step is to round the sum of the total to the closest 100 which is 800. The students should report that they collected 800 pennies.
19	>	This exercise is a comparison of two decimals in the hundredths place, 0.46 and 0.13. Since 0.46 is greater than 0.13, the greater than symbol (>) is correct: 0.46 > 0.13
20	C	This is an exercise involving multiples. The set of numbers that has only multiples of 3 is (c) 6, 9, 12
21	<	This is a comparison exercise involving fractions. By finding a common denominator of eighths for both fractions, it can be determined that 1/4 is equivalent to 2/8. And then, 2/8 is less than 5/8 so, the less than sign is correct: 1/4 < 5/8
22	D	This exercise is to measure the angle using a protractor. The angle measures (d) 35°.
23	365	The quotient of 1,825 ÷ 5 = 365. Any method can be used to solve.
24	B and E	This exercise involves identifying lines of symmetry. The moon (b) and the plus sign (e) show lines of symmetry such that the placement of the line makes both sides exactly the same.

     LumosLearning.com   ◄

Question No.	Answer	Detailed Explanation
25 PART A	90 min	This is a two-step exercise involving time. The first step is to find the sum of the time in minutes it takes to get from the classroom onto the bus (15 min.) and from the school to the state capital (1 hr. 15 min.) which must be converted to minutes (75 min.) ; 15 min. + 75 min. = 90 min.
25 PART B	9:00 A.M.	The second step is to work backward from the time they must arrive (10:30 A.M.) and subtract 90 min (or an hour and a half). They must leave no later than 9:00 A.M.
26	1,159	This is an exercise involving the subtraction of two four-digit numbers. The difference between the total number of sandwiches made in April (2,591) compared to March (1,432) must be identified: 2,591 - 1,432 = 1,159. The answer is 1,159 sub sandwiches.

27 — This is an exercise that involves generating a number pattern that follows a given rule using an In/Out table. The rule is "Multiply by 3". Three numbers were omitted that needed to be identified in the table. Those numbers are in bold. 7 x 3 = 21; 10 x 3 = 30; 15 x 3 = 45

IN	1	2	7	**10**	12	**15**
OUT	3	6	**21**	30	36	45

Question No.	Answer	Detailed Explanation
28	D	This exercise involves finding the sum of mixed numbers with like denominators. The sum is 3 2/3 since the sum of the whole numbers (1 + 2) totals 3 and the sum of the fractions (1/3 + 1/3) totals 2/3 .

29 — This exercise involves identifying the relative size of measurements within a system of units (ounces to pounds). A conversion table is to be completed to convert 4 ounces to pounds.

OZ.	lb.
16	1
32	**2**
48	3
64	4

Question No.	Answer	Detailed Explanation
30 PART A	$2\frac{5}{8}$	This is a two-step exercise involving the multiplication of whole numbers and fractions. In the first step, the product of 7 and 3/8 is to be identified: 7 x 3/8 = 21/8 = 2 5/8.

Question No.	Answer	Detailed Explanation
30 PART B		In the second step, the total number of whole pizzas that is needed is to be identified. 2 5/8 is found between 2 and 3. To be sure there is enough, 3 pizzas should be ordered.
31	432	This exercise is the multiplication of two two-digit numbers. 36 dozen cupcakes is to be identified. 36 x 12 = 432 cupcakes
32	B	This exercise is to identify the model that best represents the addition of fractions with the same denominators. B is correct as it shows 2/5+ 3/5

2/3 is best shown with: 3/5 is best shown with: to give the sum of 5/5:

Question No.	Answer	Detailed Explanation
33	C	This exercise involves identifying equivalent fractions. The set of fractions in which all the fractions are equivalent to 1/4 is (c) 2/8, 3/12, 4/16. That is because 1/4 x 2/2 = 2/8; 1/4 x 3/3 = 3/12 and 1/4 x 4/4 = 4/16.
34	C	This exercise involves the addition of three four-digit addends. The sum of the peanuts packaged on Monday (1,265), on Tuesday (2,019), and on Wednesday (1,932) is to be identified. 1,265 + 2,019 + 1,932 = 5,216
35		This exercise involves finding a whole number quotient and remainder using the properties of operations in a standard algorithm. The correct numbers that are to be identified are in each box:

Question No.	Answer	Detailed Explanation
36	A and D	This exercise involves understanding the sum of fractions as a decomposition of a fraction in several ways. 5/6 can be decomposed as (a) 1/6 + 1/6+ 1/6+ 1/6+ 1/6 and (d) 1/6 + 2/6+1/6+ 1/6.

Question No.	Answer	Detailed Explanation
37		This exercise involves plotting a point on a number line to represent a decimal in the hundredths. The correct position of 0.76 on the number line is on top of the 7th vertical marker .70 .71 .72 .73 .74 .75 .76 .77 .78 .79 .80
38	60°	This exercise involves recognizing the measurement of a circle and considering a fraction of the circle. One sixth of a circle is to be determined. The equation $360° \div 6 = 60°$ can be used to solve. The measurement of each angle is 60°.
39	A and D	This exercise involves identifying acute angles in two-dimensional figures. The right triangle (a) and parallelogram (d) each have at least one acute angle.

Notes

LumosLearning.com

End-Of-Year Assessment (EOY) - 2

Student Name: **Start Time:**
Test Date: **End Time:**

Here are some reminders for when you are taking the Grade 4 Mathematics
End-of-Year Assessment (EOY).

To answer the questions on the test, use the directions given in the question. If you do
not know the answer to a question, skip it and go on to the next question. If time permits, you may
return to questions in this session only. Do your best to answer every question.

---

1.   **Enter your answer in the box.**

       Find the difference. 8,632 - 3,955 = [   ]

2.   Tino brought crackers to share with the kids at chess club after school. The box
       contained 59 crackers. If there were 8 kids in the chess club, what is the largest
       number of crackers each kid can receive? How many will be left over?

       Ⓐ Each kid gets 3 crackers with 7 left over.
       Ⓑ Each kid gets 6 crackers with 11 left over.
       Ⓒ Each kid gets 8 crackers with 0 left over.
       Ⓓ Each kid gets 7 crackers with 3 left over.

3.   The MacGregor family paid for several repairs to their home. The repairs are listed
       in the table below:

fence	$70
kitchen sink	$35
front door	$45
deck	$75

       PART A

       What was the total cost of all the repairs?

       Enter your answer in the box. [$]

PART B

Three workers completed the four repairs. Each worker earned the same amount of money. How much money did each worker earn?

Enter your answer in the box. | $ | | per worker

4. Jenna can walk 1 mile in 20 minutes. If she can hold that pace and does not stop, how many hours will it take her to walk 6 miles?

PART A

Complete the conversion table to identify how many hours it will take Jenna to walk 6 miles at a 20 minute per mile pace.

mile	minutes
1	20
___	40
4	___
5	100
6	___

PART B

How many hours will it take Jenna to walk 6 miles at the 20 minute per mile pace?

Ⓐ 1 hour
Ⓑ 1.5 hours
Ⓒ 2 hours
Ⓓ 2.5 hours

5. Write the correct comparison symbol (<, >, or =) in the box.

$$\frac{3}{3} \boxed{} \frac{1}{8}$$

6. Round 3,708 to the nearest hundred.

Enter your answer in the box.

7.   Select the choices that are factor pairs for the number 36.

     Ⓐ 1 and 36
     Ⓑ 2 and 16
     Ⓒ 3 and 13
     Ⓓ 4 and 9
     Ⓔ 5 and 8
     Ⓕ 6 and 6

8.   During art class, Ms. Rees instructed the class to draw a right angle as part of a drawing of a house. Which should the children draw if they want to make a right angle?

Ⓐ

Ⓑ

Ⓒ

Ⓓ

9. $\frac{4}{10}$ is equivalent to what decimal?

Check the box above the decimal that is equivalent to $\frac{4}{10}$.

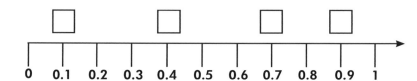

10.   Enter your answer in the box

Find the product. 5,127 x 3 = [   ]

11. The measure of ∠EFG is 120°. The measure of ∠EFL is 80°. Find the value of y.

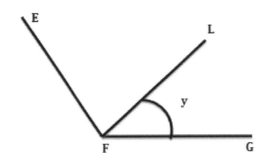

PART A

What equation best shows how to find the value of y?

Ⓐ 120° + 80° = y
Ⓑ 120° + y = 80°
Ⓒ 120° - 80° = y
Ⓓ y - 120° = 80°

PART B

What is the value of y?

Enter your answer in the box.

12. What is the quotient of 500 ÷ 50?

Ⓐ 450
Ⓑ 10
Ⓒ 100
Ⓓ 1000

           LumosLearning.com   ▶

13. Which two figures have at least one set of perpendicular lines?

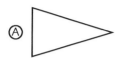 (A)

(B)

(C)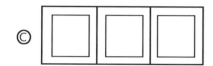

(D)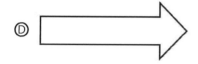

(E)

14. Enter your answer as a simplified fraction in the box.

$$\frac{4}{9} + \frac{3}{9} = \boxed{\phantom{\frac{--}{--}}}$$

15. Which two of the following numbers are prime?

4, 11, 25, 40, 61, 74

(A) 4
(B) 11
(C) 25
(D) 40
(E) 61
(F) 74

16. Nate's father needs 162 feet of wooden boards to build a deck. He can only buy boards that are 5 feet long.

PART A

Chose and write the numbers and symbols into the box to complete an equation that can be used to find t, the number of boards Nate's father needs. Each symbol may be used more than once or not at all.

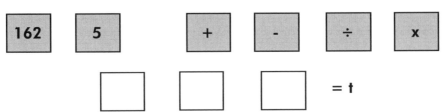

| 162 | 5 | | + | - | ÷ | x |

☐ ☐ ☐ = t

PART B

What is the fewest number of 5 foot long boards that Nate's father needs to buy?

Enter your answer in the box. ☐ boards

17. Write the correct comparison symbol (<, >, or =) in the box.

three hundred seventy-two ☐ 300 + 70 + 2

18. What is the next multiple of 8?

8, 16, 24, _____

Ⓐ 30
Ⓑ 31
Ⓒ 32
Ⓓ 40

19. Find the sum.

$3\frac{1}{4} + 2\frac{2}{4}$

Ⓐ $5\frac{3}{8}$

Ⓑ $5\frac{3}{4}$

Ⓒ $5\frac{3}{16}$

Ⓓ $6\frac{2}{16}$

LumosLearning.com   ▶

20. There are 4 adults in Rebecca's family. Her family is planning a trip to Paris. It costs $1,456 in airfare for each adult to fly from New York City to Paris. What is the total cost for 4 adults to fly from New York City to Paris?

Enter your answer in the box. | $

21. Find the sum of the fraction model.

Ⓐ $5\frac{1}{2}$

Ⓑ $5\frac{3}{4}$

Ⓒ $5\frac{3}{16}$

Ⓓ $6\frac{2}{16}$

22. Sam is 4 times as old as Frank. Frank is 5 years old.

PART A

Drag and drop the numbers and symbols into the blanks to complete an equation that can be used to find x, Sam's age. Each symbol may be used more than once or not at all.

Drag and drop the numbers and symbols into the correct order.

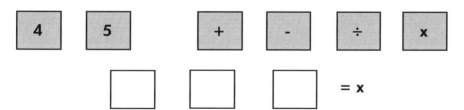

PART B

How old is Sam?

Enter your answer in the box. | | years old

23. The Cruz family was having lasagna for dinner. The father ate $\frac{1}{6}$ of the lasagna, the mother ate $\frac{2}{6}$ of the lasagna, and the child ate $\frac{3}{6}$ of the lasagna.

PART A

Which equation best shows how much of the lasagna the Cruz family ate?

Ⓐ $\frac{1}{6} + \frac{1}{6} + \frac{1}{6}$

Ⓑ $\frac{1}{6} + \frac{1}{6} + \frac{1}{6} + \frac{1}{6} + \frac{1}{6} + \frac{1}{6}$

Ⓒ $\frac{1}{6} + \frac{2}{6} + \frac{3}{6}$

Ⓓ $\frac{3}{6} - \frac{2}{6} - \frac{1}{6}$

PART B

How much of the lasagna did the Cruz family eat?

Enter your answer in the box as a fraction.

$$\frac{}{6}$$

24. There were 1,224 guests attending a sales conference. Eight guests sat at each table. If all of the tables were filled, how many tables were there at the sales conference?

Enter your answer in the box. _____ tables

25. Catharine wanted to sketch a right triangle to make a diagram of a skateboard ramp. Which triangle should she chose to make the sketch of the skateboard ramp?

Ⓐ

Ⓑ

Ⓒ

Ⓓ

26. Jackie has 4 goldfish. Mark has three times as many goldfish as Jackie.

PART A

Use symbols and drawings to show how many goldfish both Jackie and Mark have.

Each oval represents 1 goldfish. Draw the appropriate number of ovals in the correct box to show how many goldfish Jackie and Mark have and cross them off from the group of goldfish below. Some or all of the ovals may be used.

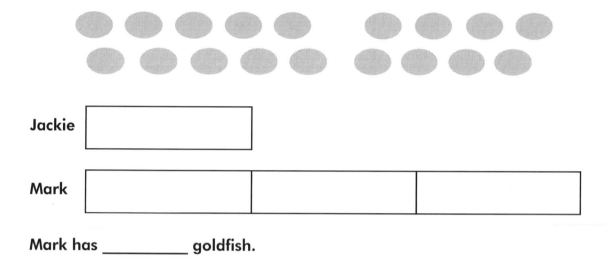

Jackie

Mark

Mark has _____ goldfish.

PART B

Which equation best shows m, the number of goldfish Mark has?

Ⓐ m = 3 + 3 + 3
Ⓑ m = 3 x 4
Ⓒ m = 12 – 4 - 3
Ⓓ m = 4 + 4 + 4 + 4

27. The principal's office is 9 meters long and 6 meters wide. What is the total floor area of the principal's office?

Enter your answer in the box. [   ] square meters

28. Enter your answer in the box.

Find the following sum: 6,941 + 3,219 = [   ]

29. **Which two angles each measure about 90°?**

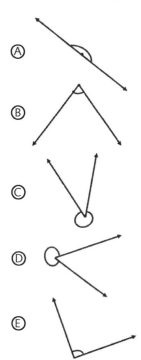

Ⓐ

Ⓑ

Ⓒ

Ⓓ

Ⓔ

30. **How many lines of symmetry does a square have?**

Ⓐ 1
Ⓑ 2
Ⓒ 4
Ⓓ 8

LumosLearning.com ▶

31. What is $5 \times \dfrac{2}{3}$?

PART A

Shade $\dfrac{1}{3}$ fraction pieces into the whole circles to best show $5 \times \dfrac{2}{3}$.
Some or all of the $\dfrac{1}{3}$ fraction pieces and whole circles can be used.

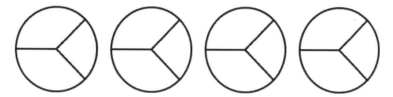

PART B

What is the product of $5 \times \dfrac{2}{3}$?

Enter your answer in the box.

32. Nineteen boys from Scout Troop 516 are going camping. Three boys can sleep in each tent. What is the least number of tents they need to bring?

PART A

Complete the table to determine how many tents the Boy Scouts need.

No. of boys	No. of tents
3	1
6	2
9	3
12	4
___	5
18	6
21	___
___	8

PART B

What is the least number of tents that all 19 Boy Scouts need if 3 boys sleep in each tent?

Enter your answer in the box. _____ tents

33. Which expression is equivalent to 3,501?

   Ⓐ (7 x 500) + 1
   Ⓑ 3,500 + (1 x 7)
   Ⓒ (3,500 ÷ 7) + 1
   Ⓓ 3,000 + 500 + 7

34. Jeremy and Meena took the same math test. Jeremy got $\frac{2}{3}$ of the answers correct. Meena got $\frac{4}{5}$ of the answers correct. Did Jeremy or Meena get more answers correct on the math test?

   _____ got more of the answers correct.

35. Max rode his bike for 3.25 miles and then stopped to eat some lunch. He finished his ride by going another 1.85 miles. How many miles did Max ride in all?

   Enter your answer in the box. [   ] miles

36. Chloe and Bethany were walking home from the bus. They decided to count how many steps it took to get from the bus to their house. Chloe counted three hundred forty-seven. Bethany counted 300 + 30 + 6.

   Who counted more steps?

   Enter your answer in the box. [   ] counted more steps

37. Each small square below is equivalent to the decimal 0.01 Compare the decimal models using comparison symbols (<, >, =).

   Enter your answer in the box.

 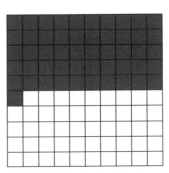

LumosLearning.com   ▶

38. Start at 41 and create a pattern with the rule "Subtract 5." Considering 41 to be the first number, what is the seventh number in the pattern?

Ⓐ 9
Ⓑ 10
Ⓒ 11
Ⓓ 12

39. Which three fractions are equivalent to $\frac{1}{10}$?

Write three fractions that are equivalent to $\frac{1}{10}$ into the boxes.

| $\frac{10}{100}$ | $\frac{2}{20}$ | $\frac{4}{10}$ | $\frac{7}{70}$ | $\frac{1}{25}$ | $\frac{10}{80}$ | $\frac{1}{1}$ | $\frac{9}{100}$ |

☐ ☐ ☐

End of End-Of-Year Assessment (EOY) - 2

End-Of-Year Assessment (EOY) - 2

Answer Key

Question No.	Answer	Related Lumos Online Workbook	CCSS
1	4,677	Addition & Subtraction; Rounding Numbers; Compare Numbers and Expanded Notation	4.NBT.4-2
2	D	Multi-step Problems; Real World Problems	4.OA.3-2
3 PART A	$225	Multi-step Problems; Real World Problems; Number Sentences	4.OA.3-1
3 PART B	$75	Multi-step Problems; Real World Problems; Number Sentences	4.OA.3-1
4 PART A	*	Units of Measurement	4.MD.1
4 PART B	C	Units of Measurement	4.MD.1
5	>	Compare Fractions; Equivalent Fractions	4.NF.2-1
6	3,700	Rounding Numbers	4.NBT.3
7	A, D, F	Number Theory	4.OA.4
8	B	Points, Lines, Rays and Segments; Classifying Plane (2-D) Shapes	4.G.1
9	0.4	Convert Fractions to Decimals	4.NF.6
10	15,381	Multiplication; Addition & Subtraction; Rounding Numbers; Compare Numbers and Expanded Notation; Place Value	4.NBT.5-1
11 PART A	C	Angle Measurement	4.MD.7
11 PART B	40°	Angle Measurement	4.MD.7
12	B	Place Value	4.NBT.1
13	C and D	Classifying Plane (2-D) Shapes; Points, Lines, Rays and Segments;	4.G.1
14	$\frac{7}{9}$	Adding & Subtracting Fractions	4.NF.3a
15	B and E	Number Theory	4.OA.4-4
16 PART A	162÷5=t	Multi-step Problems; Real World Problems	4.OA.3-2
16 PART B	33	Multi-step Problems; Real World Problems	4.OA.3-2
17	=	Compare Numbers and Expanded Notation	4.NBT.2
18	C	Number Theory	4.OA.4

* See detailed explanation

LumosLearning.com   ▶

Question No.	Answer	Related Lumos Online Workbook	CCSS
19	B	Adding & Subtracting Fractions	4.NF.3c
20	$5,824	Multiplication	4.NBT.5
21	A	Adding & Subtracting Fractions	4.NF.3a
22 PART A	4 x 5= x	Number Sentences; Real World Problems	4.OA.1-2
22 PART B	20	Real World Problems	4.OA.2
23 PART A	C	Adding & Subtracting Fractions	4.NF.3d
23 PART B	$\frac{6}{6}$	Adding & Subtracting Fractions	4.NF.3d
24	153	Division	4.NBT.5
25	B	Angles	4.G.2
26 PART A	*	Real World Problems	4.OA.2
26 PART B	B	Real World Problems	4.OA.2
27	54	Perimeter & Area	4.MD.3
28	10,160	Addition & Subtraction; Rounding Numbers; Compare Numbers and Expanded Notation; Place Value	4.NBT.4-1
29	B, E	Angle Measurement	4.MD.5
30	C	Symmetry	4.G.3
31 PART A	*	Multiplying Fractions	4.NF.4b-2
31 PART B	$3\frac{1}{3}$	Multiplying Fractions	4.NF.4b-2
32 PART A	*	Multi-step Problems; Real World Problems; Number Sentences	4.OA.3-1
32 PART B	7	Multi-step Problems; Real World Problems; Number Sentences	4.OA.3-1
33	A	Division; Multiplication; Addition & Subtraction; Compare Numbers and Expanded Notation; Rounding Numbers	4.NBT.6-2
34	Meena	Equivalent Fractions	4.NF.1
35	5.1 miles	Measurement Problems	4.MD.2-2
36	Chloe	Compare Numbers and Expanded Notation	4.NBT.2
37	>	Compare Decimals	4.NF.7
38	C	Patterns	4.OA.5
39	*	Equivalent Fractions	4.NF.1

* See detailed explanation

End-Of-Year Assessment (EOY) - 2

Detailed Explanations

Question No.	Answer	Detailed Explanation
1	4,677	This exercise is to find the difference between two four-digit numbers. 8,632- 3,955 = 4,677
2	D	This is a single-step word problem involving division where remainders must be interpreted. Since 59 ÷ 8 results in a quotient of 7 and a remainder of 3, then (d) each kid gets 7 crackers with 3 left over.
3 PART A	$225	This is a two-step problem involving addition and division with whole numbers. In the first step, the total cost of all the repairs is $70 + $35 + $45 + $75 = $225.
3 PART B	$75	In the second step, the amount each of the 3 workers get can be calculated using the equation $225 ÷ 3 = $75. Each worker receives $75.
4 PART A		This is a two-step exercise involving a conversion table to find a ratio and the conversion of minutes to hours. In the first step, the conversion table is to be completed to show how long it would take Jenna to walk 6 miles at a 20 minute per mile pace. The correct numbers on the conversion table are shown in bold and bigger font size:

mile	minutes
1	20
2	40
3	60
4	**80**
5	100
6	**120**

Question No.	Answer	Detailed Explanation
4 PART B	C	In the second step, the time in minutes (120) it took her to walk 6 miles is to be converted to hours. The answer is (c) 2 hours.
5	>	This exercise is a comparison of fractions with different denominators. Since 3/3 equals one whole, 3/3 is greater than 1/8, so the greater than symbol (>) is correct. 3/8 > 1/8

     LumosLearning.com   ▶

Question No.	Answer	Detailed Explanation
6	3,700	This exercise involves rounding. 3,708 rounded to the nearest hundred is 3,700. The zero in the tens place causes the hundreds digit to remain a 7.
7	A, D, F	This is a factoring exercise that requires three correct responses. The three factor pairs for 36 are (a) 1 and 36, (d) 4 and 9 and (f) 6 and 6 because each factor pair when multiplied together equals 36.
8	B	This exercise involves identifying right angles in two-dimensional figures. The only figure showing a right angle is (b).
9	0.4	This exercise involves identifying the decimal notation for a fraction with a denominator of 10. The decimal that is equivalent to 4/10 is 0.4 The box above 0.4 should be checked.
10	15,381	This exercise involves multiplying a four-digit number by a one-digit number using strategies based on place value and properties of operations. The product of 5,127 x 3 = 15,381
11 PART A	C	This is a two-step problem involving the recognition of angles as additive. In the first step, the equation that best shows the value of y is required. As ∠EFG is 120°, and ∠EFL is 80°, the equation that best shows the value of y is (c) 120° - 80° = y.
11 PART B	40°	In the second step, the value of y is to be determined. 120° - 80° = 40°, so y = 40°.
12	B	This exercise involves recognizing that in a multi-digit number, a digit in one place represents ten times what is represents in the place to its right. 500 ÷ 50 = 10, because 500 is ten times as much as 50. (50 x 10 = 500).
13	C and D	This exercise is to classify two-dimensional figures based on the presence of perpendicular lines. Only the series of three squares and the arrow have at least one set of perpendicular lines. Hint: Look for right angles.
14	$\frac{7}{9}$	This exercise involves the addition of fractions with like denominators. The sum of 4/9 and 3/9 equals 7/9 .
15	B and E	This exercise is to determine prime numbers. The two prime numbers on the list are (b) 11 and (e) 61 as their only factors are 1 and themselves. All the other numbers are composite and have other factors than 1 and themselves.

Question No.	Answer	Detailed Explanation
16 PART A	162÷5 = t	This is a two-step problem involving the division of whole numbers where remainders must be interpreted. In the first step, an equation must be created finding t, the total feet of wood boards needed. The correct equation is 162 ÷ 5 = t.
16 PART B	33	In the second step, the fewest number of boards needs to be determined. Since 162 ft. ÷ 5 results in 32 and a remainder of 2 ft., 33 boards are needed.
17	=	This exercise is a comparison of three-digit numbers as a number name and expanded form. The number name three hundred seventy-two equals 372. The expanded form of 300 + 70 + 2 should be converted to 372. This makes the number name and the expanded form equal, so the equal sign (=) is correct: three hundred seventy-two = 300 + 70 + 2
18	C	This is an exercise involving multiples. The next multiple of 8 is (c) 32.
19	B	This exercise involves the addition of mixed numbers with like denominators. 3 1/4 + 2 2/4 = 5 3/4
20	$5,824	This exercise is a one-step word problem involving multiplying a four-digit number by a one-digit number. The given numbers require a general strategy based on place value or properties of operations. Airfare for 4 adults at $1,456 (4 x $1,456) is $5,824.
21	A	This exercise involves the addition of mixed numbers with like denominators using a fraction model. The fraction model shows 1 3/4 + 3 3/4. The sum of the fraction model is (a) 5 1/2.
22 PART A	4 x 5=x	This is a two-step problem that requires representing a multiplicative comparison as a multiplication equation with a symbol for the unknown number. In the first step, an equation is to be created to represent the statement, "Sam is 4 times as old as Frank." Frank is 5, with x being Sam's age. The correct equation is 4 x 5 = x.
22 PART B	20	The second-step is to solve for how old Sam is. Sam is 20 years old.
23 PART A	C	This is a two-step problem involving the addition of fractions with the same denominators. In the first step, the equation that best represents how much the Cruz family ate is to be selected. The correct answer is (c) 1/6 + 2/6+ 3/6 .

Question No.	Answer	Detailed Explanation
23 PART B	$\frac{6}{6}$	The second step is to determine the amount of lasagna that was eaten as a fraction. Only the numerator is required. The amount eaten was 6/6.
24	153	This exercise is a one-step word problem involving dividing a four-digit numbers by a one-digit number. The quotient is a whole number. 1,224 guests divided by 8 tables (1,224 ÷8) is 153 tables.
25	B	This exercise is a word problem requiring the classification of two-dimensional figures based on the presence of a right angle. Only B shows a triangle with a right angle.
26 PART A		This is a two-step problem involving multiplying to solve a word problem involving a multiplicative comparison by using a drawing and an equation. In the first step, the number of goldfish that Jackie and Mark have are represented by ovals and are to be moved into the rectangles so that Jackie has 4 goldfish and Mark has 12 (4 in each rectangle): Jackie Mark
26 PART B	B	In the second step, the corresponding equation is to be selected in which m represents the number of goldfish Mark has. The correct answer is B, m = 3 x 4.
27	54	This is an area problem in which the length (9 meters) and the width (6 meters) are given. The equation that can be used to solve is 9 x 6 = 54. The principal's office has a floor area of 54 square meters.
28	10,160	This exercise is the addition of two four-digit numbers that requires a standard algorithm as the numbers do not suggest any obvious mental strategy. The sum is 10,160.
29	B and E	This exercise involves estimating the measurement of an angle. The two angles that are about 90° are (b) and (e). Although (d) also appears to be a right angle, the indicator shows that it is the reflex angle that is being measured.

Question No.	Answer	Detailed Explanation
30	C	This exercise involves recognizing lines of symmetry for a two-dimensional figure. A square has 4 lines of symmetry.
31 PART A		This is a two-step exercise involving the multiplication of a whole number and fractions using a fraction model. In the first step, 1/3 fraction pieces are to be dropped into the whole circles to show 5 x 2/3 . This requires placing 10, 1/3's into the whole circles.
31 PART B	$3\frac{1}{3}$	In the second step, the product of 5 x 2/3 is to be determined using the visual model, which is 3 1/3.
32 PART A		This is a two-part word problem involving whole numbers in which remainders must be interpreted. In the first step, a conversion table is to be completed to determine the ratio of boys per tent (3:1). The three missing parts are shown in bold in the table below:

No. of boys	No. of tents
3	1
6	2
9	3
12	4
15	5
18	6
21	**7**
24	8

Question No.	Answer	Detailed Explanation
32 PART B	7	In the second step the least number of tents needed is to be determined. As there are 19 boys, 7 tents would be needed.
33	A	This exercise is to find a whole-number quotient and remainder with four-digit dividend using place value and the relationship between multiplication and division. 7 x 500 = 3,500 and then adding 1 gives the dividend of 3,501 resulting in the expression (7 x 500) + 1

Question No.	Answer	Detailed Explanation
34	Meena	This exercise is a simple word problem involving a fraction comparison. The fraction of correct answers each child got on their math test is to be compared. As 4/5 (Meena's score) is greater than 2/3 (Jeremy's score), Meena got more of the answers correct.
35	5.1 miles	This exercise is a word problem involving distance and the addition of simple decimals. Max rode his bike in two segments, so the addition sentence 3.25 + 1.85 can be used to solve. Max rode 5.1 miles in all.
36	Chloe	This exercise is a word problem involving the comparison of two multi-digit numbers given in various forms. The task is to compare the steps Chloe took as the number word three hundred forty-seven to the steps Bethany took which was 300 + 30 + 6 in expanded form. Three hundred forty-seven = 347, and 300 + 30 + 6 = 336, so 347 is greater. Chloe counted more steps.
37	>	This exercise is a comparison of decimals to the hundredths using a decimal model. The model on the left shows 0.54 and the model on the right shows 0.51. The correct comparison symbol would be greater than (>) because 0.54 is greater than (>) 0.51.
38	C	This exercise requires extending a pattern following a given rule. The pattern or rule is subtract 5, starting at 41. The seventh number in the pattern is 11; 41 − (5 x 6) = 11 or 41 - 5 - 5- 5 - 5 - 5 - 5 = 11.
39		This exercise is to recognize equivalent fractions. The three fractions that are equivalent to 1/10 are 10/100, 2/20 , and 7/70 .

Notes

Notes

Lumos StepUp™ is an educational App that helps students learn and master grade-level skills in Math and English Language Arts.

The list of features includes:

- Learn Anywhere, Anytime!

- Grades 3-8 Mathematics and English Language Arts

- Get instant access to the Common Core State Standards

- One full-length sample practice test in all Grades and Subjects

- Full-length Practice Tests, Partial Tests and Standards-based Tests

- 2 Test Modes: Normal mode and Learning mode

- Learning Mode gives the user a step-by-step explanation if the answer is wrong

- Access to Online Workbooks

- Provides ability to directly scan QR Codes

- And it's completely FREE!

http://lumoslearning.com/a/stepup-app

About Online Workbooks

- ◆ When you buy this book, 1 year access to online workbooks included

- ◆ Access them anytime from a computer with an internet connection

- ◆ Adheres to the New Common Core State Standards

- ◆ Includes progress reports

- ◆ Instant feedback and self-paced

- ◆ Ability to review incorrect answers

- ◆ Parents and Teachers can assist in student's learning by reviewing their areas of difficulty

Course Name: Grade 4 Math Prep

Lesson Name:	Correct	Total	% Score	Incorrect
Introduction				
Diagnostic Test		3	0%	3
Number and Numerical Operations				
Workbook - Number Sense	2	10	20%	8
Workbook - Numerical Operations	2	25	8%	23
Workbook - Estimation	1	3	33%	2
Geometry and measurement				
Workbook - Geometric Properties		6	0%	6
Workbook - Transforming Shapes				
Workbook - Coordinate Geometry	1	3	33%	2
Workbook - Units of Measurement				
Workbook - Measuring Geometric Objects	3	10	30%	7
Patterns and algebra				
Workbook - Patterns	7	10	70%	3
Workbook - Functions and relationships				

LESSON NAME: Workbook - Geometric Properties

Elapsed Time: 01:19

Question No. 2

What type of motion is being modeled here?

Select right answer

- ◯ a translation
- ◯ a rotation 90° clockwise
- ◉ a rotation 90° counter-clockwise
- ◯ a reflection

[Previous question]   [Next question]

Report Name: Missed Questions

Student Name: Lisa Colbright
Cours Name: Grade 4 Math Prep
Lesson Name: Diagnostic Test

The faces on a number cube are labeled with the numbers 1 through 6. What is the probability of rolling a number greater than 4?

Answer Explanation

(C) On a standard number cube, there are six possible outcomes. Of those outcomes, 2 of them are greater than 4. Thus, the probability of rolling a number greater than 4 is "2 out of 6" or 2/6.

A)		1/6
B)		1/3
C)	Correct Answer	2/6
D)		3/6

Lumos Learning
Developed By Expert Teachers

PARCC
Practice Tests
ENGLISH LANGUAGE ARTS

★ **2** Performance Based Assessments (PBA)

★ **2** End-Of-Year (EOY) Assessments

★ Includes Mobile Access

(((**tedBook**)))

★ Detailed Explanations And Answer Key

PLUS **ONLINE WORKBOOKS**
WITH HUNDREDS OF PRACTICE QUESTIONS

Adheres to Common Core State Standards
www.LumosLearning.com

Available

• At Leading book stores

• Online www.LumosLearning.com

Made in the USA
San Bernardino, CA
05 January 2015